CURIOUS CONSTRUCTIONS

A PECULIAR PORTFOLIO OF FIFTY FASCINATING STRUCTURES

WRITTEN BY
MICHAEL HEARST

ILLUSTRATED BY
MATT JOHNSTONE

chronicle books·san francisco

CURIOUS CONTENTS

A WORD FROM THE AUTHOR

I'm fascinated by constructions. Especially curious ones. And by constructions I mean . . . wait, surely I don't need to explain to you what the word "construction" means, do I? I do? Okay, I'll try. But this gets complicated. If you are prone to confusion, just turn the page. If not, then here goes: In essence, a construction is something that is built or made. At least, that's one of the definitions—the one that's most important to this book. But by that definition a construction could be just about anything! An airplane shaped like a beluga whale, a banana vending machine, a device that makes your bike sound like a galloping horse. (Look them up; they exist.) Unfortunately, that's way too much for a 102-page book. Another definition of construction (as written in the Macmillan Dictionary) is "A building or other large structure." For example: the International Space Station, the Eiffel Tower, the Great Wall of China, etc. (Yes, a beluga airplane is also a large structure, but I'm purposefully leaving out vehicles since they fit so nicely into their own category.) Okay, now that you know why I've chosen what I've chosen, it's time for you to turn the page, for real.

— MICHAEL HEARST

ARECIBO OBSERVATORY

Listen closely! If Earth had an ear, you would probably find it in the rainforests of Puerto Rico, and it would probably look something like this. Welcome to the Arecibo Observatory. Back in the 1950s, an astronomer named William Gordon, along with a team of scientists and engineers from Cornell University, had an idea for building a radio telescope so powerful that it could pick up signals not just from Earth's ionosphere, but also from regions of space billions of miles away! They were told it simply couldn't be done.

On a remote, hilly location in Puerto Rico, south of Arecibo, construction began in 1960 . . . and just over three years later, the telescope detected its first signals! Today, the Arecibo dish is the world's largest and most sensitive telescope. It picks up radio signals, which radiate from *all* objects in outer space and travel in every direction, including toward Earth. The signals bounce off the 40,000 panels on the dish, which is 1,000 feet (305 metres) in diameter, and are then collected by the domed reflector system dangling 450 feet (137 metres) above.

The dish remains stationary, but the domed reflectors can be moved to change the direction from which the observatory receives signals. To this day, the Arecibo Observatory has discovered some pretty impressive things, including:

- the precise number of days it takes Mercury to orbit the sun (there are 59 days in a Mercury year).
- a binary pulsar (two neutron stars that orbit around a common center).
- the first exoplanets (planets outside of our own solar system).
- a group of one-eyed Martians who are listening back at us with their own giant radio telescope.

P.S. That last one isn't true, but you knew that. The Arecibo Observatory, however, was used in 1974 to broadcast a radio message toward a star cluster 25,000 light-years away. We're still waiting for a response.

BUT WHAT *IS* A RADIO TELESCOPE?

Glad you asked. With a regular "optical" telescope, astronomers study light waves. Similarly, with a radio telescope, scientists study radio waves. The radio waves are detected by the telescope and then sent to computers that translate the signals and turn them into maps and images.

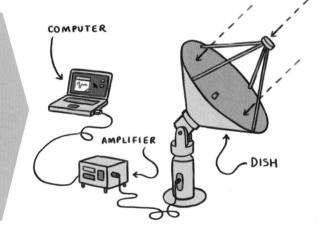

COMPUTER

AMPLIFIER

DISH

THINK FAST!

China is currently building an even larger radio telescope . . . the Five-Hundred-Meter Aperture Spherical Telescope (a.k.a. FAST) in Guizhou Province. As the name suggests, the telescope dish will be 500 meters (1,640 feet) wide, and will be three times more sensitive than the Arecibo Observatory.

BERKUT OIL RIG

We humans have a big dependency on oil. And with such big dependency comes big construction. Although there are thousands of oil rigs around the planet, the Berkut oil rig is currently the largest, standing 472 feet (144 metres, or roughly equivalent to a 50-floor building) and weighing over 200,000 tons (181,436 tonnes). This monster of a machine can slurp up 4.5 million tons (4 million tonnes) of crude oil in a year. To boot, it's been constructed to handle some of the harshest subarctic conditions, such as temperatures of −47° Fahrenheit (−44° Celsius), or a wall of ice 6.5 feet (2 metres) thick. In theory, it can also survive a magnitude 9 earthquake and a 52-foot (15.8-metre) wave. President Vladimir Putin was on hand (via video link) for the platform's opening in June 2014. He commented, "Thanks to projects like Berkut, we can now utilize richer—but difficult-to-access—oil fields, open up new production, and overall strengthen the socioeconomic development of our country's most important region: the Far East." And to that I comment, "Boo."

The Berkut oil rig is a "gravity-based structure," which means that the concrete legs are directly anchored into the seafloor. The main platform contains mud pumps, drilling equipment, compressors, generators, firefighting equipment, pedestal cranes, and even living quarters.

SO, WHO'S BATHING IN ALL THIS OIL?

Berkut was a group effort. (Which certainly makes a $12 billion project easier on the wallet.) The oil is shared between America, Japan, Russia, and India.

LUBE JOB

Working on an offshore oil rig is no bed of roses—after all, you *are* stuck on a platform in the ocean. However, wages are often around $300 per day, with annual salaries at approximately $47,000. During the off-season, you can spend all your earnings on gas for your car.

BIOSPHERE 2

About 30 miles (48 kilometres) north of Tucson, Arizona, is a structure with 6,500 windows—a giant greenhouse for humans called Biosphere 2. Essentially, it's meant to act like an artificial Earth. But wait? Then where's Biosphere 1? You're in it! Earth *is* Biosphere 1. Of course, if we humans were ever to colonize another planet (say Mars), we would need to build a new biosphere so that we could grow food, recycle water, and, uh, breathe. That's exactly what oil millionaire John P. Allen had in mind when he funded the construction of Biosphere 2 back in the 1980s. Within the confines of this massive 3-acre (1.2-hectare) system are a rainforest, desert, wetlands, and even a mini ocean complete with beach and coral reef. How amazing is that? And for two years, eight scientists were sealed inside its glass walls to see if, in fact, humans could survive in an artificial Earth. Unfortunately, on several occasions, outside assistance was needed to keep the team healthy (e.g., pumping in extra oxygen). Not to mention the group split into sides at one point, feuding over how to manage the Biosphere. The general public largely considered the experiment a failure. But perhaps this was based on the idea that Biosphere 2 was some sort of survival game. Most scientists will agree that an experiment is always a success, so long as we learn something. And in the end, with Biosphere 2, we learned that maybe we're not quite ready to colonize Mars.

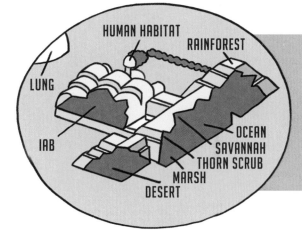

Today, the University of Arizona uses Biosphere 2 for research. You can also take a tour of the facility for $20 ($13 for kids!). However, you may want to bring a few tanks of oxygen with you, just in case you get locked in.

PIZZA PARTY!

At one point, Biosphere resident Jane Poynter decided to try to make a pizza. She had to grow wheat and then harvest the wheat to make dough. She also had to raise a goat and milk the goat to make cheese. In all, it took her four months to make the *whole-wheat goat-cheese pizza*.

BOB BURNQUIST'S MEGA RAMP

Pro skater Bob Burnquist's childhood dream was to one day have a skate ramp in his backyard. Thankfully, he now owns 12 acres (4.9 hectares) of farmland in Southern California. *And on his farm* he has dogs, cats, goats, rabbits, a turtle, and, oh yeah, the world's largest skateboard ramp! By large, we're talking LARGE. To be precise, it's 360 feet (110 metres) long (longer than a U.S. football field) and 75 feet (23 metres) tall (about the size of an eight-story building.) Basically, it's large enough to make even Tony Hawk nervous. After dropping in, skaters can quickly reach speeds of up to 55 miles (88.5 kilometres) per hour, whereupon they shoot over a 70-foot (21-metre) empty gap (with just a trapeze net below). After soaring through the air, and hopefully touching down on the other side, they can ride up a massive 30-foot (9-metre) quarterpipe and launch 20 feet (6 metres) above the top of the ramp (that's 50 feet [15 metres] above the ground). Mind you, this is no regular skateboard ramp . . . this is what's called a mega ramp! *Mega* for obvious reasons. And for just $280,000, you can have one in your backyard, too.

ALTHOUGH MEGA RAMPS WERE USED FOR BMX IN THE 1990S, THE FIRST SKATEBOARDING MEGA RAMP WAS CONCEIVED IN 2002 BY PROFESSIONAL SKATER DANNY WAY. DANNY ALSO HOLDS THE RECORD FOR LONGEST JUMP, AT 79 FEET (24 METRES), AND HIGHEST AIR, AT 23.5 FEET (7 METRES). ONE TIME, USING A MEGA RAMP, DANNY JUMPED THE GREAT WALL OF CHINA! (SEE PAGE 34.)

CATHEDRAL TERMITE MOUNDS

Who said curious constructions could only be made by humans? What about a beaver dam or a spider web? Take a walk through northern Australia, and you may see some of the strangest structures on the planet . . . engineered by insects! Cathedral termite mounds, built by the cathedral termite, can be found scattered across the flat, arid landscape, reaching heights of more than 13 feet (4 metres). The tiny insect workers build their castles out of mud, plant matter, termite saliva, and feces. Ew! The mounds are incredibly strong, which keeps the colony safe from rain and predators. The mound's vertical shape allows air to circulate upward, helping the termites at the base to stay nice and cool, even when it's oppressively hot outside (as is often the case in Australia). Strangely, however, there is no opening at the top—instead, the mound is porous so that heat can escape through the walls. The worker termites are constantly maintaining the mounds. Sort of a never-ending job. Perhaps when they finally go to sleep at night, they dream about constructing even *larger* mounds. Wait, termites don't sleep?

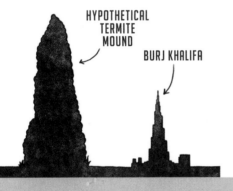

HYPOTHETICAL TERMITE MOUND

BURJ KHALIFA

TERMITE VS. MAN

If you compare the size of a termite to the size of a human, our equivalent to a cathedral termite mound would be a mega skyscraper, nearly twice the height of the Burj Khalifa in Dubai.

WHY THE TOWER OF POWER?

One million termites living together underground is one hot and stale environment. Therefore, these insects have evolved to construct vertical columns to allow plenty of ventilation. And they still get to live underground. Nifty!

TRUE OR FALSE?

1. Cathedral termite mounds may vary in color.
2. Modern cathedral termite mounds are equipped with digital thermostats to keep the inside temperature just right.
3. Cathedral termite mounds contain miniature pipe organs, which can be heard on Sundays at 7:30 a.m., 9 a.m., and 10:30 a.m.

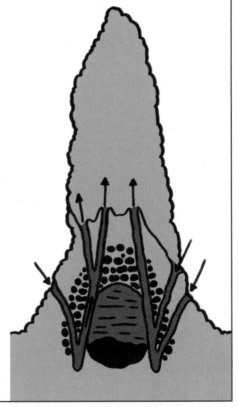

Answers 1. T (It depends on the color of the dirt.); 2. F; 3. F (Sorry, had to go there.)

CONEY ISLAND PARACHUTE JUMP

LOCATION **BROOKLYN, NEW YORK**

Paris has its Eiffel Tower. Pisa has its leaning tower. Brooklyn has its defunct parachute jump. Originally built for the 1939 New York World's Fair in Flushing Meadows Park, Queens, this former amusement ride was relocated to Brooklyn's Coney Island in 1941, where it became part of Steeplechase Park. For a mere 40 cents (25 cents for kids), you could sit in a canvas seat and get hoisted by a cable to the top of this 250-foot (76-metre) tower. After a half second of taking in the view, the cable would release and you'd parachute down along several guide wires. *Wheeee!*

Retired navy commander James H. Strong designed an early version of the parachute jump as a means of training military paratroopers. But when crowds started to gather to watch, James saw the dollar signs and decided to modify the parachute jump into an amusement ride. The ride stayed active for 25 years, until Steeplechase Park closed its gates in 1964. Although the rest of the park was demolished, it was decided that the open-frame steel structure of the parachute jump was too expensive to tear down, so it was simply left to rust. In 1989, the tower was granted landmark status by the city of New York, and soon thereafter received a new paint job and fancy blinking lights. Today you can buy a T-shirt from any Brooklyn tourist shop (yes, they now exist) with a screen-printed image of this nonoperational amusement ride.

SHOOT, WHERE'S THE CHUTE?

Recently, there has been talk of bringing the ride back to life. Unfortunately, modern safety standards would likely keep that from happening. I suppose, instead, you'll just have to parachute from an airplane.

ODE TO THE PARACHUTE JUMP

What could be more poetic
than an amusement ride of yore?
People from across America
driving to the Brooklyn shore
to get the thrill of their lives
making their parachute jumps.
While the ones below got their thrills
looking up at people's rumps.

SAFETY SECOND

Despite riders being buckled in by only a small leather harness, during its time in operation, the parachute jump had a perfect safety record. Occasionally a cable would get caught, leaving someone suspended for a few hours. But that's about the worst of it. The same cannot be said for Coney Island's 90-year-old Cyclone roller coaster, which has seen at least two deaths and countless injuries. In fact, I still have a headache from the time I rode it five years ago.

12

DESERT BREATH

Should you happen to wander the Sahara Desert in Egypt not far from the Red Sea, and should you happen to come across a series of cone-shaped protrusions and indentations spiraling out and increasing in size, you may scratch your sunburned head and wonder what UFO landing site you've stumbled upon. Perhaps this curious construction would make more sense if you saw it from an airplane? Perhaps not. Alien theories aside, the creators of Desert Breath are three Greek artists—Danae Stratou, Alexandra Stratou, and Stella Konstantinides (collectively known as D.A.ST. Arteam). They built this site-specific project with help from the Egypt-based company Orascom Development in 1997. Desert Breath still exists today, though much of it has disintegrated back into the land, which the creators say is part of the project—a measure of time!

BUT WHY IS IT HERE?

A VERY BRIEF POEM FOR DESERT BREATH

Because aliens love the desert! (Okay, I'll stop with the aliens.) According to D.A.ST. Arteam, this location was chosen for Desert Breath to represent the infinity of the sea coexisting with the infinity of the desert. Unfortunately, the body of water that originally sat in the center of Desert Breath has evaporated, making this representation a little bit trickier to see. But still.

UFOs have landed here!
Or is it an alien flowchart?
Wait, you say this is simply
human-made, site-specific art?

HOW BIG IS IT?

IT TAKES UP ABOUT 1 MILLION SQUARE FEET (92,903 SQUARE METRES). THAT'S PRETTY DARN BIG. IN ALL, THERE ARE 89 CONES, AS WELL AS 89 CONICAL DEPRESSIONS. IT CAN EASILY BE SEEN FROM GOOGLE EARTH. GO AHEAD, LOOK IT UP: N 27°22' 49.4", E 33°37' 55.9".

DYAR TUNNELS

LOCATION WASHINGTON, D.C.

Some people collect postage stamps; others build model airplanes. Dr. Harrison Gray Dyar Jr., an entomologist who lived from 1866 to 1929, liked to dig tunnels. And by tunnels, we're talking multiple staircases, long hallways, and passages that reached a depth of 32 feet (9.7 metres) and extended 200 feet (60.9 metres) from his Washington, D.C., home. Measuring 6 feet by 6 feet (1.8 metres by 1.8 metres), and lined with white enamel brick, these curious tunnels ultimately went nowhere. The labyrinth was one of Dyar's big secrets. That is, until it was finally discovered in 1924 when a truck fell through. Oops! By then, Dyar had moved across town, where he likely read headlines such as the *Washington Post*'s, "Old Tunnel Here Believed to Have Been Used by Teuton War Spies and Bootleggers"! Eventually Dyar fessed up, stating that it had just been a hobby. The shafts still exist today. However, they are sealed up with concrete.

DAY JOB

Because digging tunnels under your house for no apparent reason doesn't pay the bills, H. G. Dyar worked for the Smithsonian. Specifically, he was honorary custodian of Lepidoptera. In other words, he studied larval insects such as moths, butterflies, and mosquitos.

BUT WHY?

There are varying reports, including an article in a 1932 issue of *Modern Mechanix* (not to be confused with *Popular Mechanics*), which states that the idea first came to Dyar when he decided to make an underground entrance to his furnace room. Apparently, the digging provided a great way to blow off steam after a hard day at work. So he simply kept on digging. Another article, in the *Washington Star*, alleges that he was digging a flowerbed for his wife. "When down perhaps 6 or 7 feet (2 metres), surrounded only by the damp brown walls of old

Mother Earth," he was "seized by an undeniable fancy to keep on going." Here I should point out that Dyar had another big secret—he had two families! Although he was married with two kids, he secretly married another woman and had three more children under the alias Wilfred Allen. It should also be pointed out that when the tunnels were discovered, copies of German newspapers were found pasted to the ceiling, often with references to German submarine activity. Hmm.